From A to Z ...

Future @Work

An Employee Survival Guide
for the 21st Century

Nick Synko

Cartoonist: Brian Narelle

Published by
Hickory Street Press
Saline, Michigan USA

Third Printing   2002
Second Printing   2000
First Printing   1999

The Team of Contributors

Cartoons:	Brian Narelle
Cover Design:	Sans Serif, Inc.
Production:	McNaughton & Gunn, Inc.
Editors:	Cathy Yuska & Donna Angle
And...	The many other contributors acknowledged on page 179

ISBN 0-9674886-0-5

Library of Congress Catalog Card Number: 99-76720

Printed in the United States of America

For further information, visit our website:

www.FutureAtWork.com

Hickory Street Press
PO Box 823, Saline, Michigan, 48176-9363 USA
Phone (734) 944-4488

Table of Contents

First Thoughts...

Why this book will help you and your company.

Successful 20th century companies long ago realized that everyone, from the receptionist who opens the front door in the morning, to the shipping clerk who closes the dock doors each evening, is a critical part of the team.

Yet, the business sections of most bookstores have row upon row of books targeted solely at company presidents, entrepreneurs and professional employees.

You may ask, as have I, what has been written to help ALL employees in a world-class business understand the critical concepts so vitally necessary for personal and corporate success? The answer, now, is *Future@Work.*

Having worked in corporate America for over twenty-five years, ten of them as a consultant, I have listened to thousands of people in management and non-management positions and have written this book as a report of the critical employee concepts necessary in the 21st century business world.

Easily arranged, from A (Attitude) to Z (Zero Defects), *Future@Work - An Employee Survival Guide for the 21st Century* provides each employee the knowledge they need to compete as strong team members in jobs and companies that will become the economic foundation of the 21st century.

On a personal note, it is my sincere desire that reading this book will provide the answers you may have been seeking for personal, career and corporate success.

If you would like to scan the topics covered in this book, you are invited to review the Table of Contents. It contains chapter titles as well as an introductory sentence explaining the contents of each chapter.

ATTITUDE

Why is managing your attitude part of your job?

It wasn't until the end of the 20th century that many companies encouraged employees to become decision makers and business team members. Being a partner in the business, not just a pair of callused hands and a strong back, became the new job description of the future.

At this same time, as employees became more involved in business teams, I began to hear conversations about keeping employee attitudes positive. Up until then, employees may have talked about attitudes, however, a person's attitude was often considered to be separate from his/her job performance.

Since I had personally struggled with the importance of keeping my attitude positive, I paid attention to these discussions.

For many years, it was easy for me to look at successful people and to write off their success to the advantages they were born with or given. Advantages, as I saw them, included: intelligence, education, family connections, personality or even one's height.

Putting these factors together, success was easy -- that is, if a person had a high IQ, had family connections, was well educated, personable and over six-feet tall.

2

All of these thoughts converted to a simple formula.

Great Advantages = Great Success

Applying this formula to me, was not comforting. "No reason to even try," I thought, "I just wasn't born lucky enough." I was of average intelligence, came from a working class family and was of average height. In every respect, I was AVERAGE!

Therefore, I wasn't accountable for being anything but -- well -- average.

However, at the same time, I had somehow acquired a fierce desire to be much more than average. "How much could I achieve if I really tried?" I needed an answer.

Eventually people I met along the path of life began to perplex me. I knew people with all the best advantages who weren't achieving much success. I also knew seemingly average people who were living abundantly successful lives.

Questions. "How could advantaged people fail? How can average people achieve such great success?"

I later concluded that successful people simply must work harder than everyone else. I called it multiplying hard work times the "advantage factor."

The formula for success became:

$$\text{ADVANTAGES} \times \text{WORK} = \text{SUCCESS}$$

That's it. It's simple. I recalled that even a great artist like Michelangelo, who had enormous artistic advantages, also painted every day in the Sistine Chapel. In his head were his advantages. In his hand and paint brush were the work.

Hallelujah! There was a chance for me. Although I did not have the skills of a Michelangelo, I sure could work harder. Working hard and enjoying it was an advantage I possessed. I'd be like Teddy Roosevelt and remind myself, "I am just an average person who works much harder than the average person." So with renewed energy, I worked and worked.

It wasn't long until I was working like crazy, and still just getting along. Success seemed as elusive as ever. "What was I missing?"

Years and many books later, I eventually found the answer. It is something I call "mental rocket fuel." For a person's physical body, fuel is: sleep, exercise, a healthy diet, lots of water, etc. Yes, physical fuel is important.

However, I had found mental fuel to be far more valuable. Using words and thoughts as mental fuel was a new concept for me. The importance of a positive attitude, enthusiasm and focusing on a can-do approach to life had not been part of my thought patterns.

Les Brown, author and popular motivational speaker, popularized the phrase, "Your attitude determines your altitude." My attitude, I came to understand, was grounding my altitude.

Part of every day, I had to admit, were negative thoughts such as: "This will never work. I wasn't that good in school. I'm not smart enough. I'm not talented enough or lucky enough."

I was using "septic-sludge" thoughts as fuel.

I was taking my advantages and multiplying them by hard work, then canceling it all by a negative attitude.

Remember what happens when you multiply by a negative -- the result is always a negative! Launch pad crash! No matter what advantages I had, no matter how hard I worked, my negative attitude was severely limiting any success.

Progress! I needed to choose a new mental fuel.

It was time to rewrite the formula for success:

$$\text{ADVANTAGES} \times \text{WORK} \times \text{ATTITUDE} = \text{SUCCESS}$$

Finally, after long years of puzzling, I had devised a formula for success that made a difference.

I was back in control! I began to refuel my mind with positive thoughts, with positive words, with positive books and audio tapes and positive people.

At the same time, I avoided negative people, negative newscasts, negative newspaper articles, negative thoughts and procrastination as if they carried a contagious deadly disease. I considered a positive thought as "rocket fuel" and a negative one as "septic sludge." I began making conscious choices as to what I would expose my mind and emotions.

The formula for achieving success, as I finally came to know it, also applies collectively for a group of employees at a company. Any group of people can have a negative attitude and get a negative result.

Any group of people can also greatly improve their chances of success by multiplying their skills, abilities and work efforts by a positive attitude.

The question we asked at the very beginning of this chapter was, "Why is managing your attitude part of your job?"

Perhaps the simplest answer is, "Which do you want fueling you, your company, and your future -- septic sludge or rocket fuel?"

Exercise

If there is a personal or work-related area of your life, in which you would like to achieve more success, you may want to try using the success formula found at the top of page 7 and answer the following questions:

ADVANTAGES	×	WORK	×	ATTITUDE	=	SUCCESS
What do you have? Make an inventory of the following: • Experiences • Strengths • Skills • Talents • Abilities • Interests • Aptitudes Be sure to consider past, present, at work and outside of work categories.		What are you doing? • Effort • Time • Patience • Action • Decisions • Solutions While thinking may be part of "doing," be sure that actions you are taking are part of this factor.		What is your attitude? • Are your thoughts positive? • Are the words you use positive? • Are you avoiding negative inputs into your life? • Are you increasing positive inputs to your day?		What exactly do you want to achieve? • Are you focusing upon a specific goal? • You may want to skip ahead and read chapters: G and X in this book.

BEFORE

Why doing "Befores" precedes the harvest.

While defining an alphabet of skills for the 21st century workplace, we also need to look back at tried and true concepts.

The second concept of work required for 21st century survival has been known for centuries to farmers. Farmers know that in order to harvest, they have to plant, water, weed and toil almost continuously. Farmers know a basic survival principle; that is, an investment of hard work is required BEFORE expecting a harvest.

However, in today's accelerated society, some of us have lost track of what I have to come to call the "Before Principle" of survival.

Today, most of us live in a world of instant entertainment on television, instant lasagna in the microwave and instant access to information on the Internet. All of this instant access has led to a habit of life that appears to be driven by the concept of, "Ask and you shall receive -- instantaneously."

It becomes easy to lose sight of the fact that untold hours of production work went into the television program, the preparation of the lasagna or the computer connections of the Internet. Work, hidden behind the scenes in each of these cases, often appears to be unnecessary. In each case, the harvest appears to be ready before work is performed.

As illustrated below, our artist seems to be waiting for an instantaneous sculpture. How long will he wait before he realizes that, no matter what he may be dreaming, the statue will only appear after the work of hammering and chiseling?

MAN, WITH HAMMER AND CHISEL, WAITING FOR SCULPTURE TO APPEAR

Unfortunately, some people bring this "I want it now, before I work" approach to the workplace. This attitude is often expressed as, "When they start paying me more, then I'll start working more." In other words, "I want instantaneous compensation."

An understanding of the "Before Principle" would reverse this logic and remind them they need to work more before they start earning or harvesting more. The farming equivalent to their pay-me-first logic is, "When this land begins to produce more crops, then I'll start working it harder!"

As with most jobs, before you can cash a paycheck you have to work. Few people are paid in advance. Likewise, you know that if you want a bigger harvest at work (a bigger paycheck), you have to do more work. You reap the rewards of your efforts.

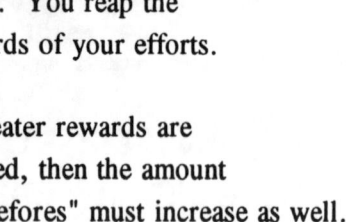
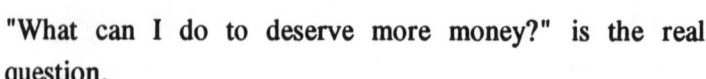

If greater rewards are desired, then the amount of "befores" must increase as well.

"What can I do to deserve more money?" is the real question.

Do you also know people who want to earn more than they contribute? They, too, have failed to plant and toil before the harvest.

Hard work is still a primary skill for the 21st century. Planting *still* comes before harvesting. Are you?

Questions

What areas of your life hasn't the harvest been as great as you would like it to be?

_____

_____

_____

What specific "Befores" could you be doing to prepare for the harvest?

_____

_____

_____

What could your company do today that would make the future more successful?

_____

_____

_____

What could you do today to help prepare for your company's future?

_____

_____

_____

CUSTOMERS

Why internal and external customers are important.

For the better part of the 20th century, the word "customer," was used to describe the company or person who purchased a company's products. The customer was often the unknown person or company "out there" to whom all internal efforts were directed.

It wasn't until the close of the century that a different type of customer was first recognized -- the internal customer. The internal customer is the person or department to whom you provide a product or a service within the company.

Two categories of customers now had to be considered - internal and external.

The respect and level of service that was formerly reserved for external customers, was now being extended to internal customers as well.

This all began when companies began having external suppliers produce some of the components they formerly manufactured within their own walls. It then became apparent that these components could be supplied by either internal or external suppliers.

The objective was, of course, to try improve quality, price and deliverables. It was at this time that internal suppliers, which no longer had a captive market for their goods or services, began to have to compete with external suppliers. Competition, then, often drove up levels of internal goods and services.

The concept of internal customers is very likely to remain an important business concept. In the ultra-competitive markets of the 21st century, unless internal customers are receiving a quality product from internal suppliers, it will be impossible for the business as a whole to provide external customers with a quality product or service.

This can seem all a little too complicated or perhaps unnecessary until we look at an example. Let's assume that we open a Ponzo's Pizza.

Our goal is to deliver a quality product and service. We soon have a few regular customers, such as the Jones family. Mr. Jones, who has several children, orders three extra-large pizzas from us every Friday evening. Mr. Jones is, of course, a valuable external customer.

This week, our driver asks Mr. Jones, "How have the pizzas been recently?" Mr. Jones replies, "I'm glad you asked. Lately, there has been burnt stuff on the bottom of the pizzas." Mr. Jones continues, "It looks like something that came off the bottom of the oven."

Upon returning to the
pizza shop, the driver
tells the baker what
Mr. Jones said.
The baker admits to
finding burnt stuff on
the bottom of the oven
at times. He explains
it comes from the
sauce, running off the
edge of the pizza into
the oven, which burns
and adheres to the crusts.

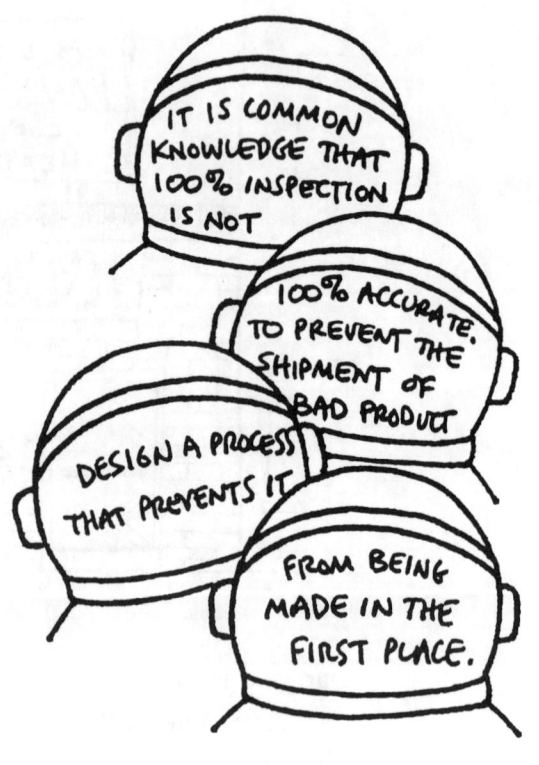

Next the baker tells
the toppings person
about the sauce
problem. The toppings
person suggests the
problem is caused by
the dough flipper
who isn't getting a
raised edge on the pizza.
She says that if there is
no edge, the sauce runs
off the pizza into the oven.

It appears the "burnt stuff" problem started with the dough
flipper, was passed on to the toppings person, on to the
baker, then to the driver and finally to Mr. Jones.

20

In this case, who needed to improve their internal process and product? Of course, the people at each stage on the pizza assembly line needed to ensure they provided their internal customer with a quality in-progress-pizza so that the external customer receives a quality pizza.

It is easy to see from this analogy that we could never satisfy Mr. Jones, our external customer, unless we first satisfied the needs of our internal customers -- the next person in the pizza assembly line. It's simply impossible. Consistently providing internal customers with a quality product or service is vital to the ultimate success of any business.

EXTERNAL
CUSTOMER

INTERNAL
CUSTOMERS

Whether you are making pizzas or car parts, you have internal customers who depend upon you doing a quality job in order for them to do a quality job.

When was the last time you asked your internal customers how you could improve the goods or services you provide them?

To extend our Ponzo's pizza story, Mr. Jones is now delighted with us and continues to be one of our best customers. We gave him his next order free. Why? Because he brought his concerns to our attention. After all, he could have said nothing and just stopped ordering from us. He could have chosen another pizza supplier.

Apply this scenario to your own job. If given a choice, might your internal customers stop ordering from you and your department? Would your internal customers choose you as their ideal internal supplier? Are you competing for their business? How do you know?

Our new motto for our Ponzo's pizza shop is:

Quality Within Our Doors
Delivers Quality to Your Door

Questions

Who are your internal customers?

_____

_____

_____

What specific questions might you ask your internal customers?

_____

_____

_____

Do employees at work treat each other with the same respect and level of service that they would give an external customer? What examples can you give?

_____

_____

_____

DO IT NOW!

Why "DO IT NOW" is the foundation for tomorrow.

If ever it is exceedingly apparent that time passes quickly, it is at the start of a new millennium. It is also obvious that we are beginning a new century brimming with potential.

However, the goals and dreams you have for this century, be they personal or professional, may often appear to exceed the time you have to devote to them. They often are -- for those who procrastinate.

For certain, people who will achieve success in the 21st century will have no more time than the twenty-four hours allotted to each of us each day. These people will NOT operate on the FALSE ASSUMPTION that others have more time and opportunity available to them. They will use the same minutes, hours and days available to us all.

A friend once said, successful people know the past is a memory and the future is filled with the beauty of dreams, yet, NOW is the biggest gift they will ever receive. That is why they call it the "present."

Whether it is wisdom from a friend or popular words from a shoe advertisement, the concept of "JUST DO IT" is full of practical advice for anyone who wants to experience the full potential of life.

One of my favorite training instructors, Bob Moawad, tells his students about a wonderful mythical island in the South Pacific called "Someday Isle." Its sister island is the even bigger "Tomorrow Isle" in the chain of isles called the "Next Year Isles." I like to tell students, "Someday, I'll take you there."

You get the point. The Isles exist only in our imagination. So tend to be our somedays, tomorrows or next years. Days turn into months, months into years and years into forgotten thoughts or "wish I would haves," or worse yet, into regrets. Perhaps the saddest phrase ever spoken is the one that begins with, "Oh, what could have been if..."

It's the people and companies who DO IT NOW who gain a competitive edge. While you may have been thinking of SOMEDAY finding a way to do your job more efficiently, your competition DID IT TODAY. They improved their work processes and lowered their cost. That allowed them to lower their prices which got them one of your best customers. While you were thinking of someday developing a better way to train new employees, your competitors got an orientation team going. They think in "Now Time."

Now their new employees are immediately more efficient, saving money and reducing scrap levels while they learn the job and preventing those all-too-often injuries experienced by new employees. Of course, you may have been thinking of doing the same thing when you got to "Next Year Isle."

My favorite calendar has
the days of each month
stacked upon each other
much like the floors of
a building. Day one of
each month is on the bottom
floor. Day two is stacked
above it on the second floor
and so on.

Arranging the
calendar in this manner
suggests that today is
the foundation for tomorrow.

We all have a list of
"someday" thoughts. We
tend to forget, however,
that **tomorrow rests upon
today.** What you will be
able to accomplish tomorrow
is the direct result of
what you accomplished today.
Think about it. What can
you start today that will
make tomorrow better?

SUNDAY	AUG 7
SATURDAY	AUG 6
FRIDAY	AUG 5
THURSDAY	AUG 4
WEDNESDAY	AUG 3
TUESDAY	AUG 2
MONDAY	AUG 1

Then DO IT NOW.
Tomorrow, DO IT NOW and
the next day DO IT NOW.

One last thought.   Thinking
without action is wasted time.
Action without thinking is
foolishness. Thinking with
action can change you, your
company and your future.
Procrastination will be the loser.
You will be the winner.

Do you operate in "NOW TIME?"

Exercise

We all have a "someday" list. From that list, what is more than a wish and clearly a desire you want to accomplish someday?

_____

_____

_____

Let's work together to begin today, to DO IT NOW rather than someday. Make a photocopy of the "Now Watch" in this chapter. On the top of the page write the desire you wrote in the space above on this page.

Next, take the photocopy of the watch and fold it several times until it is approximately one inch square. Put it in your shoe. Whenever you are reminded of the discomfort in your shoe, think about what you could DO NOW to begin working on your goal.

Keep the paper in your shoe as long as it keeps you in a DO IT NOW mode.

EDUCATION

Why educating is more than talking.

Check each of the following statements as true or false.

1.   The more a company spends on education, the lower their turnover rate. ☐ T   ☐ F

2.   During the first 90 days of employment, scrap rates go down and efficiency goes up dramatically with a well-constructed job skills training program. ☐ T   ☐ F

3. Training new workers in job skills is everyone's responsibility. ☐ T ☐ F

Of course, all these statements are true and worth reminding ourselves of from time to time. As the speed of change and technology development accelerates, training may be THE competitive edge of the 21st century. Unfortunately. Yes, unfortunately, because many employees see training as someone else's job. Many employers see training as something to be done in spare time -- which, of course, is never available. Therefore, unfortunately, the competitive edge that effective training offers is never attained.

This raises important questions anyone who might train a new employee in job skills should be able to answer. They are: "What is different about education or training that produce results? How do you get the competitive edge that well-trained employees offer a company?" Clearly said, "How do you deliver training that 'sticks to the brain' rather than goes in one ear and out the other?"

For example, let's assume you are responsible for training new employees in your department. In your opinion, the new employees don't seem to be learning the required job skills. Is it because the employees are not capable of learning, or is the root cause of the problem ineffective teaching methods?

Experience has taught me that when education or training fails, it is often because the instructor did too much talking.

When employees are subjected to an endless flood of words, almost everything goes in one ear and out the other. Try as we might to listen, when it comes to learning new job skills, the majority of us DO NOT learn by listening. That is, we are not auditory learners.

Most of us learn far more effectively when visual aids such as actual products or equipment, sketches, diagrams, and pictures are included along with instructions. Words alone are just not as effective as illustrations and words. The age old saying, "a picture is worth a thousand words," is true in this situation.

That said, there is even a more effective way to teach than by only using words and pictures. Combine words, pictures and actions. Have the student complete the actual task several times, as the instructor offers guidance. This is the most complete and effective way to educate.

TELL — SHOW — DO

I have found that being able to train coworkers effectively is an important job skill for all employees. That's because in today's business world, most experienced employees have the opportunity to train new employees. This may include a quick on-the-job instruction or a more involved lesson. Knowing the basics of education will make every educating or training attempt easier for instructors and a more effective learning experience for students.

Let's take a look at each step:

1. TELLING - A series of step by step verbal instructions;

2. SHOWING - A series of step by step visual illustrations;

3. DOING - The opportunity to perform the task several times while receiving feedback.

For training that "sticks to the brain," skilled educators TELL, SHOW **AND** DO. The competitive edge of providing employee training that "sticks," is a simple 1-2-3 step process.

One final question. What should you do if you are the student and these three training steps are not being used?

The answer, try: 1) asking for detailed instructions, 2) offering to make an illustration or to complete a sketch or diagram with the instructor, and 3) asking for the opportunity to complete the task (several times) while receiving feedback.

Start practicing this new skill with the exercise found on the next page. Since learning is so often in the doing, I encourage you to complete this exercise.

Exercise

Identify a task that you may have to explain to a new
employee. Design a three step process that includes:

1.   Verbal instructions

        _____

        _____

        _____

        _____

2.   Appropriate step by step illustrations

        _____

        _____

        _____

        _____

3.   The chance to perform the task with feedback.

        _____

        _____

        _____

        _____

Practice using the 1-2-3 Tell-Show-Do approach on this
single task and expand its use to other tasks as the
opportunities become available.

FACTS

Why aren't people listening to what you have to say?

When we reach the year 2999, there may be space colonies on other planets, rocket transportation in every garage and work completed at the speed of thought. To be sure, what will be happening in 1000 years is difficult to know -- with one exception. That exception is in regard to unchangeable facts. The children of that day will be taught $1 \times 2 = 2$ and that the earth is basically round. Facts remain the same, unarguable and predictable, even a thousand years from now.

Opinions, on the other hand: A) are often disregarded, or B) may lead to endless debate.

Therefore, whether in schools, in research or in business, decisions are routinely made upon as many facts as can be gathered. When it comes to decision making, facts are heavy artillery. Opinions are, well, popguns.

To illustrate the importance of using facts in business discussions, let's begin by asking a few hypothetical questions. If you were visiting Germany, what language would you need to speak? Of course, German. What if you went to China? The answer -- Chinese or Mandarin.

Now, what language would you need to speak if you were going to a fictitious country called Decision Land? The answer -- Facts. This is the language spoken in the land where all important decisions are made.

In a foreign land, you should be prepared to speak their language. If you speak Chinese in Germany they won't listen. Opinions, similarly, when spoken in Decision Land also tend to be ignored.

This reality was brought home to me years ago. While working at a manufacturing plant in Indianapolis, Indiana, I heard a manager tell an employee, "I really don't care about your opinions! I want the facts." No doubt this employee walked away frustrated and perhaps the manager was a bit harsh. Yet, if I were in this manager's shoes and had to make important decisions using either facts or opinions, I know which one I would choose.

All too often, I talk to employees who complain that no one listens to them. When I explore why they aren't being heard, I often hear them speaking the wrong language. They are speaking opinions. To be listened to, they needed to take the time to dig out the facts, to collect data,

HERE'S WHAT I FOUND...

to make specific observations and to document the details. In other words, "Facts rule!"

There is a second situation where the use of facts is absolutely critical. Never is the absence of facts so noticeable as when I hear people debating a topic again and again and failing to reach consensus. I am often asked how to resolve such a situation. The answer is to stop and get the issue out in the open. If necessary, modify the meeting agenda to allow time to address the specific disagreement in detail.

44

Then follow these four steps:

1. **State the team's objective.** Begin by writing the goal of the discussion, word for word, on flip chart paper.

2. **Outline key points of each side.** Next, ask each participant to individually identify his/her important points. Write responses on flip chart paper for everyone to see. To encourage participants to listen to differences of opinion, randomly ask people to summarize opposing viewpoints.

3. **Involve everyone in seeking a solution based upon facts.** Take the spotlight off the people directly involved in the disagreement by asking other people to contribute. Begin to separate facts from opinions. Assign information gathering tasks that may turn opinions into facts.

4. **Work toward consensus.** Generate alternatives that build upon areas of agreement. Make sure everyone is listening to each other's viewpoint. Try to find win-win solutions that everyone can support.

The next time you are
about to offer an opinion,
stop and take the time to
collect the facts first --
that is, if you truly want
to be heard. Only then
will you be able to answer
a question that is frequently
asked in Decision Land,
"How do you know?" When
asked this question, begin
your answer by saying,
"The facts are..."
Then you are speaking
their language, and will
prevent potential conflict
before it ever arises.

Exercise

To practice separating facts from opinions, identify the following statements as either true or false.

1. _____ The foreign country directly south of Detroit, Michigan is Cuba.

2. _____ There are fifty states in the United States.

3. _____ Florida is geographically east of Wisconsin.

4. _____ The White House was originally painted gray.

5. _____ You can tell the temperature by counting cricket chirps.

6. _____ Twenty-five years later, studies show students from the best colleges do best in life.

7. _____ The original Levi blue jeans were brown.

8. _____ The word "salary" originates from the money owed sailors at the end of a voyage.

9. _____ Moses took two animals of each species on the ark.

10. _____ The man who invented ear muffs also invented the first anti-tickle belt which rendered the wearer completely tickle-proof.

Answers may be found on the next page.

Answers to the exercise on page 47.

---

1. False, the first foreign country south of Detroit is Canada.

2. False, technically there are forty-six. Virginia, Pennsylvania, Kentucky and Massachusetts are commonwealths.

3. False, parts of Wisconsin are east of Florida.

4. True, until 1812.

5. True, count the number of chirps in 14 seconds and add 32 to determine the Fahrenheit temperature.

6. False, attitude is the differentiating factor.

7. True, they were made of brown tent cloth (jene fustian) from Genoa, Italy.

8. False, it comes from the fact that some Roman soldiers were paid in the commodity they protected, salt. A soldier who was a poor worker was "not worth his salt."

9. False, it was Noah.

10. True, the inventor of both was Chester Greenwood.

GOALS

How goals can help define your future.

It is probably safe to say that no one accidentally sailed around the world. I just can't imagine a sailor, who has conquered all 24,901 miles (40,075 km) of this extraordinary challenge, saying, "Well, I'm not really sure how it happened. I just went for a walk one day along the beach with my inner tube, and well..."

Those people, teams and organizations of the last century that accomplished great deeds began with great goals.

People or organizations just don't wander to success. It will be just as true in the 21st century. Having a specific goal in mind is the first step when accomplishing any task of merit.

While others wish and wait, great achievers plot a course and work toward their goals.

I'll admit most of us are not going to set a goal to circumnavigate the world. Perhaps a goal of not becoming lost in the woods, is far more likely. Whether you are navigating the woods or a part of your life, goals can keep you from walking in those seemingly endless circles we all experience from time to time.

As I have observed people, it is interesting to me that everyone has goals, whether they realize it or not. Some people have goals to do "not much." Others have goals to do something extra. Different people, different goals.

A person who sets a goal to spend his hours doing as little as possible, soon establishes a "not much" pattern that saturates his life. He wastes the skills, talents and abilities he possesses and watches his life turn into "not much."

Perhaps you have also noticed such a person always seems to blame his lack of success on others. It is just easier to blame others than to say, "I don't have constructive goals I am working toward."

Yet, the person who establishes a goal to do more than expected, to help others more than expected, to think about ways to improve things more than expected, establishes a pattern of personal excellence. Excellence becomes routine, because it is his goal and habit to do so.

A few years ago, *USA Today* published a major study of "Why Teams Fail." According to the report, the number one reason for failure is not having a clearly established goal. No goal, no focus, no progress!

Although the *USA Today* study primarily concerned teams, what was learned certainly applies equally well to individuals. Failure happens when teams or individuals do not have clear goals, frequently change goals or fail to be accountable for their goals. Again, no goal, no progress.

Each day we have a choice. Do you want to be a person who sets a goal to do "not much" and end up with just that, or, do you want to be a person who sets specific goals and receives more and more of life's rewards?

Should you be using more of your skills, talents and abilities to achieve goals that are important to you and your life?

"The journey of a thousand miles begins with one step." Likewise, it can be said, "The life of many successes begins with one goal, then another, then another..."

Exercise

What are your goals for today, for this week, for this month, for this year, for your life?

Are your goals written down somewhere? Would it help to carry them with you each day? If so, you may want to take time to complete a list of goals.

	Goals for Work	Goals for You	Goals for Your Family
For This Day	● ● ●	● ● ●	● ● ●
For This Week	● ● ●	● ● ●	● ● ●
For This Month	● ● ●	● ● ●	● ● ●
For This Year	● ● ●	● ● ●	● ● ●
For a Lifetime	● ● ●	● ● ●	● ● ●

HABITS

Why you inevitably are what you repeatedly do.

Have you ever stopped to ponder why you sometimes act or think as you do? The answer could be as simple as becoming aware of your habits.

Habits appear when you do the same thing or think the same way once, then twice, then day in and day out. A habit that was at first unnoticeable, soon becomes as unbreakable as chains which surround you. Struggle as you may, the habit has got you.

The small actions or thoughts that form habits are at first almost unnoticeable, that is, until they become so ingrained, they are nearly impossible to break. Eventually, your habits become so much you that you might not even recognize that there are alternative actions or thoughts available.

Now I am not suggesting that habits are necessarily all bad. Habits can indeed be very positive. Trying to find something positive to say when others aren't being so understanding, arriving to work on-time each day without racing in the door or making notes so that you don't forget things you should remember are terrific habits to develop. Positive comments, arriving a little early and keeping a notebook of things to do, if done often enough, become in

many ways, you.
Like grains of sand,
none alone amounts
to much, yet together,
your habits define
who you are.

Isn't it true that
our actions speak
louder than our
words? Don't
others define you
by your actions?

Naturally, on the other hand,
joining into the negativity
when people are gossiping,
or continually arriving late for work,
or forgetting things you should have remembered are also
small actions that establish the patterns of your life and
define your reputation.

Small actions, done often enough, add up to impenetrable
habits that control you and your actions over a lifetime.
Good habits produce good results. Bad habits...

That is why it is important, from time to time, to stop and
ask yourself, "Is this the way I want to continue? If I do
this or think like that a hundred more times, will I establish
a positive or a negative habit? Is this who I want to be?"

Likewise, think of a
few of the dozens of
routines that are
part of your every day.
Are these positive
actions and thoughts you
want to reinforce?
Or, conversely, are
today's thoughts and
actions ones you may
want to stop now
before they become
hard to break habits?

You also want to ask
others to answer these
same questions about you.
Habits have a way of
camouflaging themselves.
No matter how hard you look,
you may be unaware of your
own habits. What is unseen
to you, may be perfectly
obvious to others.

For those habits that you would like to replace, consider
taking the following step: Find a positive opposite activity,
and when tempted into your bad habit, replace it. For
example, when tempted to be negative about the day, find
something sincerely positive to say. Then, say it.

If the negative habit you would like to eliminate is too much television, when tempted to watch TV, replace it with a walk. The key to changing habits is to replace negative habits with positive opposites and to refocus on the positive.

Focusing on the negative habit will only get you more of it.

You tend to become what you think and talk about.

Focusing on what you choose to replace it with works the same -- you will get more of the positive replacement activity as well.

The choice is yours to make dozens of times a day. The choices you make will determine whether your life in the 21st century will be in a stream of positive or negative habits.

Exercise

List habits of yours you would consider to be positive.

_____

_____

_____

_____

_____

_____

What habits would you like to change?

_____

_____

_____

_____

_____

Identify positive replacement activities for each habit you would like to change.

_____

_____

_____

_____

_____

IMPROVE CONTINUOUSLY

Why "good enough" isn't.

The early years of the 20th century were hallmarked by phrases like, "If it ain't broke, don't fix it." As we begin the 21st century, DOING & IMPROVING are part of every job.

The phrase, "If it ain't broke, don't fix it," is itself, broke. Today, successful businesses would say, "If it ain't broke, talk to others, pool your ideas and see if you can make it

61

better, faster, easier, with less waste -- before someone else does!" Repeatedly doing your job better, faster and easier again and again is a fundamental part of 21st century business.

Years ago, there was never much concern over doing your job better. You were simply expected to show up on time and do as you were told. That seemed to be more than enough.

Then business became global. Trade boundaries no longer protected jobs. Words like NAFTA and GATT became more than international free trade agreements affecting someone else in some foreign country. They began to affect your company, your job and you personally.

As a result of these agreements, competition heated up. Competitors from foreign lands, perhaps companies you never even heard of before, started bidding on contracts your company had held securely for years. Job stability and security no longer existed unless you were the best in the world.

Many companies soon realized that "good enough" really wasn't. Unlike in the 20th century, in today's ultra-competitive business world, companies have found survival to be a very real issue. For most of the 20th century, companies were expected to be around for generations of families. People often worked where dad or mom did.

Today, the future isn't secure unless you, and each employee and your company, are the best in the world. Today, just doing your job means you, along with others, are also responsible for the continuous improvement of what you do. Jobs in the 21st century require everyone to DO and IMPROVE CONTINUOUSLY, if they want to survive.

Did you ever stop to wonder where will it all end?

The honest truth is it won't end. Ever. Becoming used to change and improvement is a 21st century survival skill. Trying to hold onto the past, to the status quo is much like trying to hold onto the wing of a jet airplane as it takes off.

Similarly, what was good enough last year is being left behind this year. What was advanced productivity or technology two years ago will be in second or third place this year.

A plant manager recently said to me with his tongue-in-cheek, "I guess I should be pleased; in spite of intense competition, we continually come in second place on every contract on which we have bid. Second place among hundreds of competitors is pretty good." Of course, they still have zero contracts for next year!

To be in first place, the number of parts produced each day last year must be increased this year. Changeovers must be completed faster and more accurately than last year. Even how you answer the phone should be improving. Details add up.

Unfortunately, if you and your company do not continuously improve, there are people in other companies somewhere in the world, who neither know you, nor care if you continue to work or not. Perhaps we all wish it wasn't so. It is.

Your company expects continuous improvement from its suppliers. Your customers expect the same from your company. You need to expect the same of yourself.

Questions

What are you doing to continuously improve yourself?

_____

_____

_____

What continuous improvement opportunities do you see within your job?

_____

_____

_____

Why is waiting for management to initiate continuous improvements "old thinking"?

_____

_____

_____

What is your company doing today to ensure it will be able to renew contracts the next time they are up for renewal?

_____

_____

_____

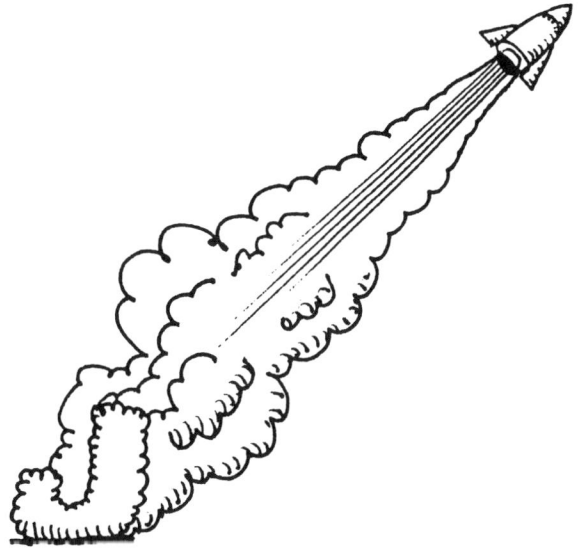

JOIN IN

How much of the load are you carrying?

Are you one of the most respected and admired people on the job? When others talk about the "best of the best" do they mention your name? To be in this elite group of "Olympians of the Workplace," you need to be committed to being the best you can be, to going the extra mile, to doing the unexpected.

On the other hand, joining in and pulling one's fair share of the load is often thought to be enough, that is, to be OK.

As in a tug-of-war rope pull, everyone pulling his/her fair share is OK. OK is the minimum. Said another way, "OK is good enough." It is, if being considered OK is acceptable to you.

Unfortunately, I often hear people in the workplace talking about the performance, or better said, the lack of performance, of coworkers.

It seems many people divide coworkers into two categories, "I wish they'd find another job," or "They're OK to work with." There is that OK level of performance again.

However, upon talking with people in a little more depth, I have found there are actually three levels of OK performance.

Let's look at each level.

I.   The Satisfactory Level - The first level of OK performance is doing a completely satisfactory job -- in all aspects. Anything less than completely satisfactory, simply isn't OK. The satisfactory performer does his/her work on time, in a quality manner, has a good attendance record and gets along with other employees. He/she is a solid performer -- the backbone of any business.

II. The Surprise and Delight Level - The second level of performance is described as those individuals who do the extras. They help others, they volunteer, they do whatever they can, and they frequently contribute more than the minimum. This level of performance is often called the surprise and delight level, because coworkers are often surprised and delighted at the extras these people contribute.

III. The Referral Level - The third level of performance is the referral level. This is the level of performance where individuals have so consistently surprised and delighted others, over such a lengthy period of time, that their coworkers would not hesitate to give them a recommendation or referral. This is noteworthy because when people give a referral, they are also putting their own reputations, as judges of character, on the line. Level three performers do not need to sell themselves. They have others saying how great it was to work with them. The referral level is considered to be the highest level of performance.

We all have a choice. If you choose level one performance, completely satisfactory, you are doing an OK job.

If you choose to be a level two performer and are known for surprising and delighting people and contributing more than expected, you are a step ahead of most people.

If you are the type of person who always wants to be known among the best, as a matter of personal pride, you will know that you have made it to the top when your coworkers are talking about you -- positively, that is.

At which level of performance would you place yourself? Why? What if everyone were performing at this level? In today's ultra-competitive world, what would the future hold for your company?

At what level do you perform? At what level does your company as a whole perform? What would your customers say?

Exercise

For each level below, list several likely examples of daily
activities you might see in a person performing at this level.

I. THE SATISFACTORY LEVEL -
II. THE SURPRISE AND DELIGHT LEVEL -
III. THE REFERRAL LEVEL -

KEEP

How consistent note-taking can improve your future.

In an era of computers and a century of advanced communications techniques, there is still a place for a pencil and a small notebook. Allow me to tell you about a job skill I learned as a management trainee for Sears.

The store manager I worked for, J.C. Johnson, was a man filled with practical advice. At the top of his list of tips for success was, "I want you to carry a pen and notebook with you at all times and to make notes of details you shouldn't forget." From his tone of voice, I knew he wasn't kidding, so I never found out what would happen if I didn't follow his instructions. Of course, he would periodically check to see if I was using the notebook or just carrying it.

I know most people don't keep a pen and a notebook with them at work. Some people make notes at their desk; however, here we are talking about a "walking about" notebook and pencil.

Few memories are so good that people don't need to make a note from time to time to make doubly sure ideas, plans, tasks or questions don't fall through the cracks. If it is important, "I forgot," is NOT an acceptable response, whether you are a senior manager or a new employee.

WITHOUT NOTEBOOK   WITH NOTEBOOK

In a world of modems, faxes, e-mail, the Internet, pocket-sized computers and who knows what is next, information overload is a reality for us all. The human brain just wasn't designed to remember the constant stream of information we all experience each day. A brain can become just as overloaded as can a computer's memory.

In response to all of these 21st century gadgets, few things are as productive and cheap (and operate without electricity) as a simple notebook.

I now know Mr. Johnson couldn't have been more correct. Taking a few notes, usually only key words, has kept me from forgetting important details and has made me seem to have a great memory and an ability to learn new tasks easily. The truth is, I just took a few notes.

Today, if I were the president of your company, I'd pass along J.C. Johnson's timeless advice and ask that every employee carry a notebook and pen. I'd even go so far as to make it a condition of employment, just as wearing an ID badge may be a condition of employment at your company. Any type of bound notebook will do. However, a scrap of paper that could easily be lost wouldn't get the job done.

A simple idea? Yes. Critical? Yes. A condition of employment? Should it be? What do you think? It is a formula for 21st century success that couldn't be more simple -- and it costs next to nothing. You just need to <u>remember</u> to carry it with you. Hey, make a note of that!

Questions

Why do or don't you carry a notebook and pen with you?

_____

_____

_____

What is on your "to do" list for today? Is it written in a notebook?

_____

_____

_____

What things are "floating around" in your head that should be on paper?

_____

_____

_____

LISTEN

Is listening more important than speaking?

A student once said, in a class I teach on communications skills, that our Creator probably favored listening over talking when He gave us two ears and only one mouth. The student went on to say that we also have two eyes which we may also use to listen with as well. Good observations.

When was the last time you heard someone relate how he really listened to someone else to try to understand what he meant and why he felt that way?

Yet, you may frequently hear people boast about telling others... so and so.

Likewise, aren't you far more proud of yourself when you say something well than when you listen well?

Yet, listening is one of the most important human relations skills we possess. Why? Here's a list of six reasons:

1.   To learn something new

2.   To make the speaker feel important

3.   To understand exactly what the speaker is saying as well as why he or she is saying it

4.   To encourage people to listen to you as well

5.   To gather the details needed to make a decision

6.   To determine what someone may or may not know so that you can fill in the gaps

Yet, as I observe people in a discussion, I frequently notice that instead of listening to the speaker, the listener is mentally rehearsing what he is going to say next, or judging and criticizing the speaker.

You will notice the same things if you observe the listener's body language or "read his face" when he is supposed to be listening.

To further observe if the listener really was listening, ask him to paraphrase what the speaker just said. Oftentimes, he has only the vaguest understanding and has missed several important details.

How, then, should you listen? Do you know someone who is a good listener? What does a good listener do that makes him a good listener?

Most books and articles on listening pair the word "active" with "listening."

Active listening involves action on your part as a listener to show you are truly hearing what the speaker is saying. To listen actively you could:

- nod, smile or frown,

- ask a clarifying question,

- take a note,

- look directly at the speaker,

- move closer (about an arm's length away),

- summarize the speaker's key points,

- or use body language: arms, hands, face, or eyes to show the speaker you are following along.

See the listening skills check list on the next page for additional action ideas on how to improve your active listening skills. If you would like to be listened to, adding some of these active listening techniques to your communications skills may well convince others to listen to you, since you are clearly listening to them.

Even in an era of technical wizardry, researchers say that technical or job skills account for less than 20% in keeping a job or in getting ahead at work. People skills count for 80%. How important do you think listening is to the 80% factor of getting along with people?

Listening Skills Checklist

1. Do you consistently set aside what you are doing and look directly at the speaker? ☐ yes ☐ no

2. Do you work at ignoring distractions and quickly dismiss interruptions? ☐ yes ☐ no

3. Do you avoid interrupting? ☐ yes ☐ no

4. Do you allow and encourage the speaker to continue by using appropriate body language? ☐ yes ☐ no

5. Do you question the speaker at appropriate points to clarify statements? ☐ yes ☐ no

6. Do you concentrate on what the speaker is saying and why she may be saying it? ☐ yes ☐ no

7. Do you identify the key point(s) of the message and make mental or paper notes? ☐ yes ☐ no

8. Do you listen thoroughly before you begin formulating your own thoughts? ☐ yes ☐ no

9. Do you restate the speaker's message and ask him if you clearly understood his intent? ☐ yes ☐ no

10. Do you evaluate or judge the message and not the speaker? ☐ yes ☐ no

Questions

Think of a person who you would identify as a very good listener. What does he/she do that makes him/her an effective listener?

_____

_____

_____

Think of a person who you would identify as the worst listener you know. What does he/she do that makes him/her a poor listener?

_____

_____

_____

When, in particular, is it difficult for you to be a good listener?

_____

_____

_____

Does the leadership team set an example by being good listeners? Specifically, how could they improve?

_____

_____

_____

MEASURE

If you don't measure you are only guessing.

In the year 2999, will a foot still be exactly twelve inches? Will the Earth still be the same distance from the sun? Will years be divided into months, weeks and days?

Will there still be a frog jumping contest every third weekend in May at the Calaveras County (California) Fair and Jumping Frog Jubilee? Most likely. It has been going on for years.

Mark Twain was one of the first to write about this world famous competition. Opinions about who has the frog that can jump the farthest are thrown about. Bragging is part of the sport. However, only one frog wins the $5000.00 first prize each year. They don't debate who has the best frog -- they get out the measuring tape. Measurement makes things much more interesting.

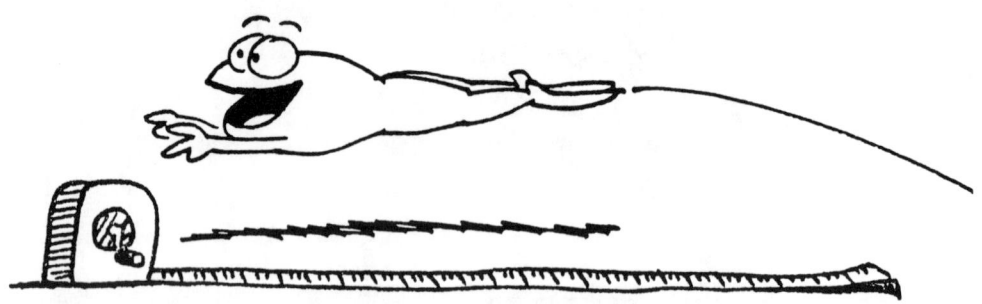

Of course, measurement changes opinions into facts, a critical difference if you are going to make important decisions about a frog's jumping ability.

Obviously, if you measure something over a period of time, you will be able to tell if the situation is improving or deteriorating. For example, are frogs jumping further in the year 2500 than they were in the 1990's? If you get serious about most things (even frogs), you find a way to measure.

At work, you may
measure production,
scrap, injuries or
customer satisfaction
levels to see if things
are improving or
deteriorating.
Once you know the facts,
you can respond
accordingly.

As work teams become
more and more sophisticated
in evaluating and
continuously improving
their processes, the
quality and quantity of
the measurements they keep
increase as well.

Let's look at three opinions versus three measurements.
Afterwards you can make your own judgment as to whether
or not the opinions are supported by the measurements.

1.   The Opinion: "My attendance is about average."
      The Measure: This person is absent or late 2-3
                     days a month. The average person
                     is absent or late 5.2 times per year.

87

2. The Opinion: "Our production is pretty good."

    The Measure: Line productivity in this area exceeds other shifts by 100 more parts, the scrap rate is 3% less, changeovers are 30% faster.

3. The Opinion: "We work as a team."

    The Measure: Last year, process-improvement teams saved the company $247,978 while improving customer satisfaction by 13.5%.

As you can see, measurements separate opinions from facts.

For example, in the world of professional sports, everyone has an opinion as to who is the best at so and so in a particular sport. What separates opinionated fans from a manager of a professional team? It's often the measurement for an infinite number of details. I once heard a radio announcer discuss a manager who pulled a hitter because of the hitter's batting average against left-handed pitchers in the second half of the game! Measurements like these are taken very seriously in a very competitive world.

People who take what they do seriously, measure. If you want to know how you, your production line or department is performing, you must be able to evaluate your performance in some measurable way.

Measurements to consider may include:

1. Internal & external customer performance
2. Departmental budgets and expenditures
3. Schedule attainment
4. Critical cycle times
5. Scrap levels
6. Savings from process improvements initiated by teams
7. Number of improved processes this year

Measurements like these and more separate the serious business competitors from those with little talent or success. All of the world-class companies I have visited have extensive and well-communicated measurement systems.

Once baseline measurements are known, it is important to set improvement goals. Opportunities to make small improvements can be found almost every day. Over time, these small improvements may yield benefits equal to those of the occasional "grand slam" improvement.

By the way, you may want to see if there are any world-class frogs in your backyard. "Rosie the Ribiter" holds the current world record with a jump of 21 feet 5.75 inches. (Further details can be found at www.frogtown.org.)

Before you leave for California next May, don't go without measuring your frog's jumping ability first. Opinions don't count in Calaveras County. They take their frog jumping very seriously. They measure.

Questions

What measurements are critical to you, your department's or
your company's long-term success?

_____

_____

_____

How are these measurements tracked and discussed at
departmental meetings?

_____

_____

_____

How do your measurements compare to the best benchmarks
within your industry?

_____

_____

_____

Is your performance improving or deteriorating? How do
you know?

_____

_____

_____

NEXT

Why some people need to be supervised.

Some of the first memories of my childhood are about shoveling coal into the furnace on a cold winter day with my dad. We always seemed to linger with the furnace door open, watching our "fireplace." Nice memories.

Yes, I miss watching the glow of the coal burning; however, a thermostatically controlled gas furnace is my choice today. The thermostat monitors the temperature and "decides" when to run the furnace and for how long.

The coal furnace, in effect, "waited to be told what to do."
The gas furnace, on the other hand, is self-regulated and
"takes the initiative to do what is necessary."

I know both types of people as well. Some people, when
working, ask themselves, "What is next?" and take the
initiative to do what is necessary. Other people wait idly
until told what to do next.

The word "next" is a simple yet powerful initiative or action
word that suggests you are open to and seeking the next
thing to do. The opposite is an "I'll wait" approach which
often means "I'll do something when I am told to do it."
"Next?" users are proactive individuals.

I remember the last time I was cleaning the basement with my two sons. The impact of using a "Next?" approach to work was clearly evident. Since, at that time, they were too young to do things on their own, they were working alongside me while I was giving them direction. I'd instruct them to: "take that box to the garage, put those boards in the corner or vacuum under the workbench."

One of my sons did exactly as I told him, yet, once the assigned task was complete, he would wait until being told what to do next or wander around or disappear. The other son would complete his task and then take the initiative to say, "What's next?"

There was quite a difference in the productivity of the two boys. If I were paying them as employees, and could choose between the two different attitudes, it is quite evident which one was more productive.

Of course, if you are new to a job, seeking general guidance and explicit direction is understandable and often necessary. If you know what to do, do it. If you aren't sure, a simple question of "What's next?" will set you apart as a person with initiative.

We began this chapter by asking a question, "Why do some people need to be supervised and others don't?" Perhaps the answer is: a coal furnace needs to be supervised and a thermostatically controlled gas furnace doesn't.

Not many homeowners are choosing coal furnaces these days, are they? How about you? If you were a company owner, which one would you choose?   Which type of employee are you?

Questions

Give an example of the types of "Next?" initiative you have seen people take.

_____

_____

_____

List examples of "coal furnace" behavior you have seen.

_____

_____

_____

How are employees trained in the broad aspects of their job and other jobs in the department?

_____

_____

_____

How are employees recognized for showing initiative?

_____

_____

_____

OBSTACLES

Are obstacles and problems the same thing?

Wouldn't we all like to have a six lane freshly paved highway to success in the 21st century?   While we all may frequently wish for a smooth road to easy success, most of us realize that those individuals known as achievers are actually great hurdlers in a life full of obstacles. Let's talk about hurdling the obstacles we all encounter in life.

Since both of my sons have been on the track team for several years, I have attended my fair share of track meets.

My favorite event is the high hurdles. At the sound of the starting gun, six runners sprint at full speed for the finish line. Then, no sooner do they get started when they encounter a waist-high hurdle in the middle of their lane.

No one stops. No one complains. No one even slows down. They just keep running "full steam ahead" and jump hurdle after hurdle. These runners want to be challenged. If they trip, fall or skin a shin, they pick themselves up, start again and keep running for the finish line.

I can't help thinking that there is an analogy in the midst of this track event. In life, some people stop and complain when they encounter an obstacle; other people are hurdlers and see the experience as a means of strengthening character.

While the concept of going through, over or around obstacles is often understood on a personal level, some people miss the connection that work can also be full of challenges that need to be looked at in a positive light.

When the reality of change sets in (or the obstacles become evident) and things aren't working as smoothly as they should, some individuals choose to say, "See, I told you it wouldn't work." They tend to look for the first glitch in the change and then put the spotlight on it, claiming that now the whole idea of changing things is a problem.

What they are
describing is an
obstacle, not a
complete failure.
They continue,
"Someone should
have figured these
problems out beforehand."
Sometimes you can't
anticipate every obstacle
on the road to success.
You prepare as best you
can, then take care of
the obstacles as they arise.

Why is the concept of getting around obstacles at work important? First, there are going to be continuous changes at work. Some changes will be initiated by you, others by teams and others by management. Of course, some changes are vitally necessary to maintain your competitive edge. The people who see every obstacle as a huge problem spend their time being very good problem finders. They are the first to tell you the change won't work.

On the other hand, there are people who see the same problems and treat these obstacles as simply hurdles on the track. It's the difference between, "See, I told you it wouldn't work," and "Let's see what we can do to solve this."

Which method are you going to choose -- problem highlighting or obstacle hurdling? For changes that are going on at work now, ask yourself, "What are the obstacles (don't ignore them) and how might we overcome them?"

It was Booker T. Washington who said, "I have learned that success is to be measured not so much by the position one has reached in life as by the obstacles which he has overcome while trying to succeed."

What personal obstacles are you facing? What obstacles are you facing at work? Want to be a hurdler?

Questions

Do you tend to see "problems" or "obstacles"? What may
be a difference in these two words as you use them?

_____

_____

_____

What obstacles have you personally gotten through at work
that have made you a more useful employee?

_____

_____

_____

What obstacles do you have at work today?

_____

_____

_____

What obstacles do you foresee at work in the future?

_____

_____

_____

PROCESSES

How to manage quality through process improvement.

How do you make a hamburger? How do you grow a garden? How do you complete your taxes each year? If you have found a method or a system for making a great hamburger, or a means to grow a garden or an easier way to do your taxes, you have a process (your own way) to complete these jobs. If you consistently do these jobs in a certain sequence while looking for better ways each time, you then have a process that you are continuously improving.

Similarly, at work, if someone wanted to learn how to do your job, you might show them your exact process. Or, you could take an "any old way will do" approach. When you are consistently doing things differently, you do not have an established process.

Likewise, since the early years of the assembly line, companies have been searching for the best process and then continuously improving it year after year. Their goal is to eliminate all waste: materials, unnecessary inventory or equipment, rework, time and lost opportunities. That is one of the ways they stay ahead of the competition and create job security.

ASSEMBLY LINE
OR
ASSEMBLY MOB?...

HENRY FORD
THE EARLY YEARS

Let's look at an example
that will explain why
focusing on processes is
so important to business
success. Let's assume you
opened a new restaurant
"Hamburger Heaven." Your
primary goal was to give
customers the best hamburger
they have ever eaten each
and every time. Whether it
was you or someone else
cooking the burgers, you
wanted to live up to your
motto, "GRE-A-A-A-<u>ATE</u>
<u>EVERY</u> <u>TIME</u>."

In order to achieve a consistently great burger, you would
want to write detailed instructions, including how to choose
beef, how to form the patties, how to set the cooking
temperature, when to turn the burgers and when to add
seasonings. These details, if exactly followed, would lead
to a consistent product. Surely, since it is your restaurant,
you would not be satisfied with everyone cooking burgers
their own way. You would want to find the best process and
stick to it.

As soon as you found the best method to cook a hamburger,
you would continuously try to decrease customer wait time,
find ways to improve quality and enhance the flavor so as to
make even better burgers faster in the future. You, of

course, would continuously be looking for ways to improve your process. If you were team oriented, you would certainly get your cooks and waiters together and ask them for ideas on how to improve their processes further.

Getting better and better means studying how you do things and finding a continuously improved process that yields better, faster and less expensive quality with less waste.

To continuously improve processes, there are two basic steps. First, people should begin doing their jobs with the same series of basic steps. For example, if you work in a manufacturing plant, first, second and third shift should set up and operate equipment the same way. If they aren't, they should take into account everyone's ideas and work together to define an optimum process.

Next, today's best method should be continuously improved. To improve processes, ask yourself a series of questions, such as:

- How do I do my job? What are the steps?

- Do other people use the same steps?

- Do I or others have short cuts or improved ways of doing things that we could share with each other?

- Are there ways to eliminate non-value added steps that add expense or waste time?

- Can movement, transfer or storage steps be reduced? As a result, can work in process be reduced?

- Can someone else in the process more efficiently complete a step?

- Can steps be done in parallel to reduce the overall process time?

- Can approval steps be delegated to someone directly in the process?

- Should the current process be scrapped and a fresh approach devised?

- Would additional steps add value or improve quality?

The benefit of having a standardized process is never so evident as when you are teaching a child to read. When working with my daughter, I began by teaching her the alphabet. As she was learning the correct sequence, initially she had her own pattern or process of reciting the alphabet, such as A, B, C, Z, E, G, D...

Can you imagine how much more difficult reading would be if we all had our own alphabet? So I continued to work with her until I began to hear A, B, C, D, E, F... the correct process.

By the year 2999, do you think there may be a new improved alphabet -- a continuous improvement on an already effective process? Perhaps, by then, "neighbor" will be spelled "nabor" just as it sounds.

Questions

What is the list of steps (or flowchart) for the processes for your job duties?

_____

_____

_____

When was the last time you or others studied your processes and found ways to continuously improve them?

_____

_____

_____

How are employees trained in flowcharting and process-improvement methods?

_____

_____

_____

What time is set aside so that employees can periodically work with others to improve processes?

_____

_____

_____

QUALITY

Is it a good part or isn't it? Don't guess!

Most of us are dedicated to doing a good job. However, we sometimes enter that gray area of indecision and ask, "Is it good enough to ship or send?" I'll predict that no matter when you are reading this book in the 21st century, you will still be wrestling with this question in one way or another. "Is it good enough or isn't it?"

So, someone offers his advice and says, "Ship it. It's good enough!" But, is it? Sound familiar?

For example, perhaps you are an assembler or machine operator and you have placed a hold tag on a few items. You are waiting for someone from the quality department to make a decision. Then time passes and quality assurance hasn't gotten there yet, and your line leader says, the parts are OK to ship. Yet, you wonder. Then the leader instructs you to scatter the questionable parts throughout the shipping container so they aren't easily noticed.

What is a person to do? In talking to a wide variety of people who have experienced similar situations, I have heard the following advice. Number one, follow your line leader's recommendation. He or she may have more experience in these areas. In such cases, according to the people I talked with, the line leader is ultimately responsible.

Next, ask if you can get a team together of leadership, line workers and department personnel to define what is an acceptable part and what isn't. Often, such a team will consult technical specifications and the customer involved to develop a product display board of unacceptable parts. They will also develop written criteria to explain why parts were rejected.

Having a display board of rejected parts in the work area will usually provide the necessary guidance to new and senior employees to help them understand what is a good part and what isn't. A visual reference or a picture speaks a thousand words of clarity when making these decisions.

I realize that developing such a display board is a time consuming task. Yet, if you consider how much time is spent discussing what is a good part and what isn't and the potential of customer complaints for shipping defective parts, a well-constructed display board is a small proactive investment in time, materials and customer satisfaction.

In the meantime, try keeping a log on your own of rejection reasons and sample parts. Doing so can help you and others in the department and will be a great start for any team who later develops such a display board.

Ask yourself: What exactly is a good part? What are examples of scrap or rework? Can others help me locate examples? How could examples be displayed? "Is it good enough to ship?" is a question that you must be able to answer. Imagine that you were on the rocket using the part you have in question. Would you take the ride?

Questions

Specifically explain what constitutes a defective part to someone unfamiliar with your product?

_____

_____

_____

What visual examples are available to clarify your words?

_____

_____

_____

Are you 100% sure that your definition of a defect is in complete agreement with your customer's definition of a defect? Explain the facts upon which your decision is based.

_____

_____

_____

How are employees encouraged to participate in the construction of visual display boards?

_____

_____

_____

ROOT CAUSE

What is a symptom? What is a root cause?

Experienced homeowners know there are the dandelions you see in the lawn, and then there are the roots of those dandelions that seem to go on forever. You know what happens if you just chop them off at the surface.

A key business concept is contained in this example. That is, in order to solve problems permanently (and to eliminate weeds) you need to eliminate the root cause.

Similarly, if you went to the beach and saw the ocean full of
the dorsal fins of sharks, you would not dare go in
swimming. What if, after a short while, the lifeguard
announced it was OK to swim since he had removed the
dorsal fins from all the sharks; would you then go in the
water?

The fins are the symptom of danger. The root cause of the
danger is the razor sharp rows of shark teeth.

118

Likewise, at work there are the obvious symptoms of problems, and then there are the underlying root causes of those problems. To eliminate problems permanently, you need to get beyond the obvious, the symptom that is showing, and get to the root of the problem.

Yet, what happens most often at work is that short-term fixes (or Band-Aids) are applied to symptoms. We all know people who rely upon "duct tape" fixes. The result: if, over a lengthy period of time, all you address are symptoms, problems keep reappearing again and again.

Sound familiar? We used to call it putting Band-Aid on top of Band-Aid to stop the bleeding. As someone said in a class recently, "We became experts at routinely fixing the same things with duct tape and Band-Aids!"

On the other hand, you will know that you have eliminated the problem at its root, if the problem is "fixed once and for all" and does not reappear.

There is a simple approach to identifying and uncovering the roots of a problem. Simply ask "Why?" repeatedly. How many times do you ask "why"? Ask until your judgment tells you that you have gotten past the obvious and reached a root cause.

For example, let's listen to a conversation between two individuals talking about a problem, a customer's complaint.

THE WHYS

Why # 1	-	Why are customers complaining?
Answer	-	Because orders are past due.

Why # 2	-	Why are orders past due?
Answer	-	Because the press is down for repair.

Why # 3	-	Why is the press down for repair?
Answer	-	The main bearing broke.

Why # 4	-	Why is the main bearing broken?
Answer	-	It broke in half due to excessive vibration.

Why # 5	-	Why didn't we replace the bearing when the vibration was first noticed?
Answer	-	Because we don't have scheduled maintenance procedures.

Why # 6	-	Why don't we have a system for scheduling repair needs?
Answer	-	Good question.

The root cause here is that scheduled maintenance needs to be completed routinely if we want to eliminate this problem once and for all. If we just dealt with the symptom of the problem, that is the customer's complaint, the likelihood is that press problems would keep reappearing all too frequently. In this case, the root cause issue, a lack of preventive maintenance, was never dealt with.

Although asking why may provide a direct path to the root of a problem, do not overlook examining how broad an issue may be. There may be numerous answers to the question of "Why?" and each answer should be considered.

What problems do you have at work that may be solved if you uncover their roots by asking a series of "why" questions? Picture a shovel with the word "why" written on the blade and keep digging deeper and deeper with this shovel until you get all of the roots.

If you can find their root causes, you may be able to eliminate the problems once and for all.

Questions

What example could you use to explain to others the difference between the symptom of a problem and its root cause?

_____

_____

_____

What problems in your work area may benefit from a search for their root cause?

_____

_____

_____

When do employees have the opportunity to thoroughly discuss the causes or roots of problems?

_____

_____

_____

How have employees been trained in using root cause analysis tools, such as the Whys or Cause and Effect diagrams?

_____

_____

_____

SPEAK UP

Why speaking up should be part of your job description.

In the 20th century, people were hired "to do their jobs." That was often interpreted to mean to follow the rules and do as they were told. One out-of-date management book I have on my shelf referred to managers as supervisors and employees as followers. Today, you would be hard pressed to find a successful company that referred to employees as followers.

Today, in the most progressive companies, employee ideas are solicited. Employees are asked to join teams, to combine their ideas with those of others and to come up with new and better ways of doing their jobs -- to speak up.

Unfortunately, there are a few people who still say, "Why should I? Isn't it management's job to think and my job to do what they tell me to do?" Fortunately, it has finally been recognized that everyone has useful ideas and the future depends upon these ideas being implemented. Why? Many of us who have lost one or a series of jobs in the 20th century realize that by helping a company to succeed, we may help ourselves to a more secure future. The illustrator for this book, Brian Narelle, said it best when he said, "If you have a better idea and don't speak up, you are following like a sheep and may end up a sweater or a lamb chop."

Personally, I have worked for a series of Fortune 100 companies. Having done so I learned that working for the biggest company did not always guarantee a secure future.

For example, I started my career at a very large retailer, then left as their market share severely declined.

Next, I was laid off at an automotive company during the massive automotive layoffs of the late 70's.

Then I joined an electronics company. Soon it began exporting more and more of its manufacturing to Asia. My job was eventually eliminated.

I found a more secure job in the domestic oil and gas industry. Soon that company was sold and dissolved.

Finally, I left an automotive supplier when it relocated across country and my family and I chose not to relocate.

When talking about my employment history, I find many others with similar experiences.

On the other hand, my father worked for one company for thirty-four years. Then he too was laid off. From his generation to mine, job security became a real issue; a secure future is no longer certain.

Therefore, if you have been at your job for years, you have good ideas. Tell someone. Please. If you are new to your job, also speak out. At times, it is the new person who isn't steeped in the patterns of a job who immediately sees improvement opportunities. Either way, junior or senior employee, use a suggestion box, ask to join a process improvement team or talk to your line leader. Speak up!

"If at first you don't succeed, try, try again" is a phrase still around today because it works! Keep speaking until you are heard. It may take several repetitions of your ideas until they are thoroughly heard or understood.

Also, remember, try to turn opinions into facts by gathering measurements to support your suggestion. Facts get people's attention.

Finally, be constructive. It is OK to point out the problems or obstacles as you see them. However, also be part of the solution.

Develop a reputation as speaking out with a new idea, just as the sheep did in the illustration in this chapter.

Note he did not complain about eating only the grass -- he suggested what he thought was a better idea! Pizza!

Questions

What should you speak up about today?

_____

_____

_____

What facts or measurements could you gather to support your ideas?

_____

_____

_____

Who else could you enlist to work as part of a team?

_____

_____

_____

TEAMS

What type of decisions should be assigned to a team?

Would you agree that other employees often have ideas worth considering? Would you also agree that five heads thinking together are better than one?

The answer is often yes, IF these five people listen to each other, use each other's skills, talents and abilities and gather facts to reach consensus-based decisions. That's because, when working together, a team is often able to spark creative ideas and solutions that surpass those of each team member.

Yet, in most work environments, it is nearly impossible to include everyone in routine decisions. There just isn't the time to continually get a team together.

I recall a team of twenty people who debated for two hours whether or not one employee should attend a one-day training program -- an investment of 40 hours for an 8 hour decision!

Let's consider another example. Imagine an Eskimo who has a superb team of huskies. If he needs to travel 100 miles he would be wise to invest the time to harness his team.

On the other hand, if he only had to travel 100 yards, he should go it alone. Harnessing a team isn't necessary.

So what is an appropriate decision worthy of a team's efforts? Conversely, when should you go it alone?

INDIVIDUAL ASSIGNMENTS

- ☐ A quick response is necessary
- ☐ Solutions are likely to be similar to past experiences
- ☐ A single person is likely to have sufficient skills to handle it
- ☐ There will be minimal direct impact on other employees

TEAM ASSIGNMENTS

- ☐ A problem or process is chronic or complex
- ☐ The situation would benefit from various perspectives
- ☐ Creative solutions and new insights are necessary
- ☐ Buy-in and commitment to a solution is critical
- ☐ Relationships between functions or people need to be built

131

Team-based decision-making can provide the extra spark of creativity that gives your company a competitive edge. On the other hand, not every decision is worthy of the time and effort of a team. To harness the team or not, you decide.

Questions

What decisions are you currently considering? List both at work and outside of work examples.

_____

_____

_____

Which of these decisions may benefit from getting a team of people together to make a better decision? Why?

_____

_____

_____

What decisions have you seen made by individuals that would have been better made by a team?

_____

_____

_____

For your work department, what set of guidelines do you use for deciding what is an appropriate decision for individuals or teams? Do you have examples in each category?

_____

_____

_____

UNDERCAPITALIZE

What are you investing in your future?

For a business, having adequate capital means there is money in reserve ready to take advantage of new opportunities. If the business is undercapitalized, money is not available for new facilities, new equipment or expansion opportunities. Lack of adequate capital for a business can mean that things remain as they are, or decline, and opportunities are lost forever.

People may also have inadequate capital. As we continue, let's assume the word "capital" does NOT only refer to the concept of storing up money. So what do you need to have stored up and have "ready to go" as opportunities arise? How about storing up skills, experience or education?

For example, imagine a flock of birds that takes a 3000 mile migratory flight every year. Now imagine if one of the birds decided to invest in himself by taking a night class in how to build his own rocket. He then saved up his bird seed and bought himself a rocket kit and now off he goes.

136

In my experience, many people think that it is solely the responsibility of the company to invest in their development. Yes, it is partially the company's responsibility to provide classroom training and opportunities to upgrade your job skills. But, again, what about you investing in you?

There are many creative and traditional ways to capitalize or invest in your future. You could take the initiative to observe and learn a new job or task in your department (on your own). Perhaps you could take the time to learn a new piece of software or how a system/program runs. You could take a class at a local college in writing skills or electronics or the basics of computers. Maybe you could even volunteer to run the company picnic or organize the United Way campaign as a means of developing your leadership ability and as a means of working with new people in the company.

All of these examples are ways of you storing up capital in you, so you won't be undercapitalized when the next opportunity comes.

Many people are already investing in the stocks they think will do best in the 21st century. While companies may come and go, and stocks will be up and down, there is a sure bet investment worth more to you than all of the Wall Street opportunities of a lifetime -- an investment in you by you. What investment could be more valuable to your future? When was the last time you "upgraded" you?

Questions

What type of investments could you be making in your personal life?

_____

_____

_____

What investments could you make in your future at work?

_____

_____

_____

What might be the result if you chose to, or procrastinated and did none of the above, ever?

_____

_____

_____

Which of these investments might you choose to begin working on immediately?

_____

_____

_____

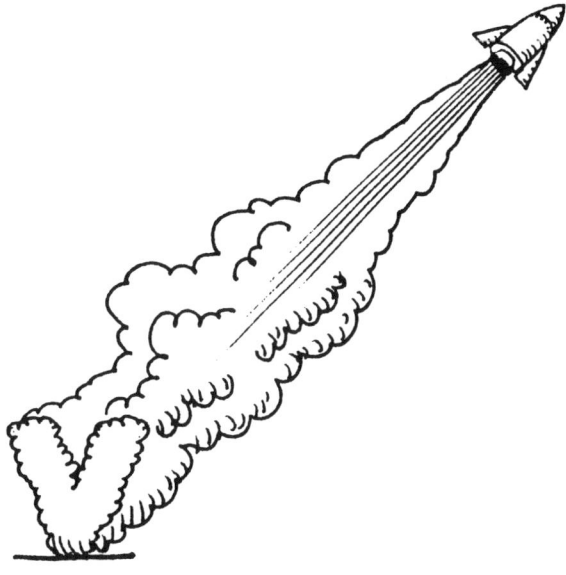

VALUES

What are your values? Are you sure?

Talking about values is often not a routine business discussion. However, I have found that the best companies often have a value-based culture. For example, late in the 20th century, one well-known company asked all employees to abide by the following values:

- Tell the truth
- Be fair
- Keep your promises
- Respect individuals
- Encourage intellectual curiosity

This set of values was meant to be kept in the forefront of everyone's mind and used to guide their daily activities. As I think about it, it seems if everyone tried to live by these values, work life, and life in general, would improve for most of us.

While developing a set of shared values at work is certainly an important topic, living by shared values begins by living a set of personal values.

Establishing a set of personal values begins by asking, what principles do you use to guide your everyday actions? What you will allow yourself to think and do is determined by your values, or lack of values, as may be the case.

Values, then, are a statement of the limitations or boundaries that you use to guide your actions. For example:

- What will you or won't you do?
- What is a right or wrong action?
- What are the rules you live by?
- What are your principles or boundaries?
- What will you take a stand for? (If nothing, are all actions acceptable?)

Answering these questions and clarifying your values will give you an inner guiding light, that others cannot help but observe. This is especially true when the "storm winds of life" begin blowing hard. Your values become your rock or anchor.

Living by a set of personal values can make a vital
difference in the path your life takes.

In order to live by values, there are two questions to
consider. First, what are your values? Second, are you
living by those values?

Knowing what you value will certainly make decision
making a whole lot easier. It will keep you within the
character boundaries you have set for your life.

141

For example, if you have values, they may include:

- telling the truth
- respecting others
- keeping your promises

Then, when someone suggests telling a small lie, your "telling the truth" value keeps you from doing so. If others are gossiping about someone, you choose not to participate because of your "respect others" value. If you promised to work on a Saturday, and at the last minute, you want to skip it, you push yourself to be there because you keep your promises. These positive actions are all examples of people knowing their values and living by them.

WHEN YOUR VALUES ARE CLEAR, WHAT ARE DIFFICULT QUESTIONS TO OTHERS, BECOME EASY DECISIONS FOR YOU.

For me, there have been times where I have not liked some of the situations or predicaments of my life. At times, it was easy to put the blame for my situation on others.

The truth is, I was much more responsible for my situation than I was willing to acknowledge. The bad decisions I had made, which led to negative consequences for me or others, I now see in hindsight as being outside my value system.

Values are then a personal set of guidelines that help you become a person of integrity. Values set you apart from others who always go along with the crowd or let their actions become misdirected. If you know people who consistently make solid decisions, it's probably because they use their values to guide their everyday thoughts and actions.

Life without values is like being in a rubber raft in a storm on the high seas. The raft is out of control and at the mercy of the waves. On the other hand, life with values is like a sailboat with a deep keel and a strong rudder that is steerable even in the roughest of conditions. Values will keep you on course even in the rough conditions you experience in your life.

143

If you haven't thought about what your values are, should you? Knowing your values is knowing the boundaries you have set for your life. Knowing your values is knowing yourself as you want to be.

Ask yourself: What do I value? What did my parents value? What do people I respect value? What values could I commit to that would help me live my life well? What about values such as: challenging your comfort zone, growing, learning, having fun, working together, producing results, respecting others, caring for family, improving yourself each day, sharing positive comments about people, talking positively to yourself, being accountable for your actions, walking your talk, listening to others, telling the truth, encouraging others, being flexible, having morals, respecting authority, etc.

Certainly, a good set of values will change and mature over time, yet a core set of beliefs will protect you from making inappropriate decisions.

The second point you need to consider is whether you live by your values. For example, you might say that you value your family, yet you don't spend time with them. You might say that you value doing your best, yet you seldom do. You might say that taking physical care of yourself is part of your values, yet you don't set aside time to exercise. In each case, you are not living by your values.

No one of us is perfect and makes every decision correctly. However, we can all start each day with an attitude of trying anew to live by the values we have chosen to govern our lives.

Do you have a set of values? Do you live by those values? Maybe you should make a list and review it daily until it is committed to memory. If you do, it will help you live your life at your best.

Questions

Who do you know who lives by and makes decisions by values? What examples could you share with others to help them understand the benefits of knowing and using values?

_____

_____

_____

What will you or won't you do? What is right or wrong as you see things? What boundaries have you set on your life? What is important enough to you that you will take a stand for it?

_____

_____

_____

Which of the above values do you live by daily?

_____

_____

_____

WIIFM

What's in it for me? -or- What's in it for us?

WIIFM -- What's In It For Me? Why do you go to work? Probably because there is something in it for you: pay, benefits, friends, a feeling of productivity, etc. These reasons are WIIFMs or what is in work for you.

As a matter of fact, everything you do at work should have a WIIFM in it, shouldn't it? If so, let's talk about what's in work for you.

First, there are short-term WIIFMs or immediately acquired gains. If you find a way to make your job easier and faster, there is clearly something immediately in it for you -- an easier job. The company also gains due to your increased productivity. This is an example of a short-term WIIFM for you and the company.

There are also long-term WIIFMs. If you find a way to reduce wasted effort, the company may be able to decrease the price it charges customers. The result may be more profits that could fund new, more productive, equipment. The consequence, increased job security, is a long-term WIIFM for you and the company.

Most people are very good at recognizing a short-term WIIFM (an easier job) and some people are even patient enough to value a long-term WIIFM (increased job security).

The most difficult type of WIIFM to recognize is called a "WIIFUS." That's, *What's In It For US*. WIIFUS thinkers realize that when we help others, we help ourselves, and conversely, when we fail to think of others, we are ultimately failing to think of ourselves.

As I observed people who were genuinely respected by coworkers, I realized that the statement, *what goes around comes around*, is the way these people operated.

148

The picture on the previous page illustrates the difference between a WIIFM (me, me me!) thinker and a team of WIIFUS thinkers.

Even if you have been watching out for yourself and have a very fancy inner tube, you will be left behind to ride out the waves when the WIIFUS ship passes you by. I'll bet the man in the WIIFM inner tube hopes that the WIIFUS ship comes around again.

"WIIFUS thinkers" have broadened their thoughts to consider ways of helping others. Then in the process of helping others, what they give to others comes around to help them. The "others" they think of may include coworkers, people outside their department, their supervisor, the company owners or stockholders or even future generations of employees.

150

There is a big difference
between focusing on WIIFM
or WIIFUS. WIIFM thinkers
tend to focus exclusively
on the word "me." WIIFUS
thinkers are more inclined
to see their connection to
others and ask, "How can
I help?"

With which type of person
would you prefer to work?
Which one would you like
to be remembered as?
Which one do you think gets
more satisfaction out of
life and actually wins in
the long-term?

What's in it for me? "Every man for himself, grab an inner
tube!" Or, What's in it for us, "Let's work together to build
a solid ship that will weather any storm."

The choice of "me" or "us" is yours to make many times
each day.

151

Exercise

What are you doing at work to help you? Make a list.

_____

_____

_____

What are you doing at work to help others? Make a list.

_____

_____

_____

Which list is longer? What should you do about it?

_____

_____

_____

X OR CROSS IT OUT

How do you eat an elephant?

How are you going to "tackle" the 21st century? Of course, one day at a time. How are you going to accomplish some of those "elephant-sized" plans you have for the 21st century? Likewise, one day at a time and one bite at a time. In order to eat "elephants," the age-old saying, "eat one bite at a time" really does work.

Many large projects "die on the vine," when they could be accomplished if they were broken down into manageable or digestible bites.

For me, writing this book was an elephant-sized project that had been "on the vine" for quite a long time. I finally began to make progress by posting an A to Z list for each chapter of the book on a flip chart in front of my desk.

154

First, I wrote "A" and then
crossed (X'd) it out on the
list. Then B, then C, etc.
It soon became, "One down,
two down, three down.
What's next?"

It was necessary to manage
my mind in this manner because
in the past, I had found large
projects to be so overwhelming
that I never got started.

On the other hand, if projects are broken into easy-to-do
steps, 1) the small steps are easier and quicker to get done,
and 2) seeing the accomplishments being "X'd" out will
motivate you to do more.   Like the snail illustrated below,
focus only on each step and try to keep your mind from
thinking about the "pyramid."

Looking at a list of crossed out tasks, as I wrote the first draft of this book, kept me on track in the moments I wanted to give up. I would think something similar to, "Look at what you've done already; *JUST KEEP GOING.*"

Do you have "elephants" in your life you would sincerely like to tackle? Here's an example of "elephant eating" that may apply to you. As you review this example, consider how you might similarly break down a large project you would like to accomplish.

Let's consider going back to school to obtain an Associates Degree in electronics. Breaking that elephant into bites, your list of small bites may include:

1. Call the technical college in your area and have them send you an information packet (which includes a campus map).

2. Review the material focusing on how to get started, the cost of one class and when the next semester begins.

3. Begin putting aside a few dollars each week to cover the total cost of one class.

4. Next drive around the campus (take the map), note where to park, which door to enter to talk to a counselor. Go inside and locate the counseling office. Then go home.

5.   Call the counseling office for an appointment. Arrange for baby sitters, etc. as necessary.

6.   During the appointment, focus on which one class you should take to begin. Make or get a list of the specific steps you need to take to get started. Don't talk about the whole curriculum. That is an overwhelmingly large elephant.

7.   Take one class and successfully complete it.

The elephant, a degree in electronics, has been turned into bites that can be easily completed one bite at a time. You would then continue taking bite-sized steps, making new lists and crossing steps off and posting your accomplishments. As you complete steps, you will see the X's begin to accumulate and to motivate you, and you will really be on the way.

As a suggestion, you may want to cross out steps using green ink out -- symbolizing "GO!" Then keep the completed lists and prominently post them where you can often see them. The progress is motivating.

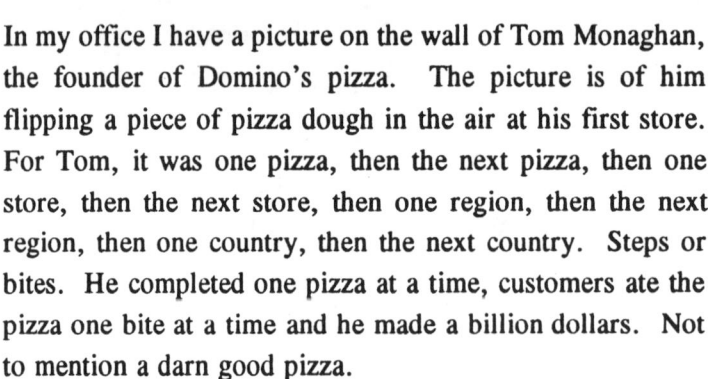

In my office I have a picture on the wall of Tom Monaghan, the founder of Domino's pizza. The picture is of him flipping a piece of pizza dough in the air at his first store. For Tom, it was one pizza, then the next pizza, then one store, then the next store, then one region, then the next region, then one country, then the next country. Steps or bites. He completed one pizza at a time, customers ate the pizza one bite at a time and he made a billion dollars. Not to mention a darn good pizza.

What elephants are staring at you. Hungry?

Exercise

List several elephant-sized projects you would like to accomplish within your lifetime.

_____

_____

_____

Which one of these projects would you like to begin soon?

_____

_____

_____

What would the steps be to accomplish this project? Be sure to keep the bites small.

_____

_____

_____

What step could you begin with tomorrow?

_____

_____

_____

YOU

Is there an "I" in the word "team"?

Have you also heard the saying, there is no "I" in the word "team"? The point is that you lose your individual identity once you are a member of a team.

My experience suggests just the opposite. Teams are comprised of individuals who must do their individual best.

Although you cannot see it, I would contend there is a capital "I" right in the middle of the word "team." Strong teams are made of strong individuals.

161

Every winning
team is a combination
of winning individuals.
Put one individual who
doesn't care on a winning
team and you now have a
losing team.

At work, I have seen
sales contracts almost
lost because of one
individual who did
not care enough to stop
making and shipping
obviously bad parts.

He simply did not care about how he affected others and their job security. If he cared enough to stop to think about it, he would have seen the "I" in team. We all know people at work who don't do their share, don't we? I frequently wonder whose job it is to talk to these individuals. Of course, the easy answer is, "It isn't my job. It's the supervisor's responsibility." But what if the supervisor hasn't noticed what is happening? What if these individuals are really good at camouflaging their actions? What if...

Many excellent employees I talk with tell me the subject of poorly performing coworkers is one they routinely discuss over a cup of coffee in the break room.

162

I know of a few excellent employees who ended up quitting and finding another job because of poor performers in their department who were continually getting away with nonperformance. They quit because they became fed up with their personal future and job security being jeopardized. A tough decision.

Strangely backward isn't it? A good person leaves and a poor performer stays. A few more rounds of those instances and it is fairly easy to predict the future of the company.

Tough questions. No easy answers.

This is one section of the book in which I have chosen not to offer an answer. However, it is the intent of the book to raise the question.

Everyone's situation is totally unique. Only you can decide what to do about those individuals on your team who are not carrying their load.

You see, once again, in yet a different sort of way, you are important to your team. If you choose to do nothing -- are you perhaps saying that your input is not important?

So what do you think should be done about poor performers? What do others in your department think? Remember -- to do nothing is also a decision.

Getting back to where we began this section, you are important. "Nothing I do around here really matters." That's a lie! There is an "I" in team. YOU do matter. The team cannot win without YOU.

Questions

What could you do to be more involved in the overall performance of your department?

_____

_____

_____

What could you do to get non-performers to carry their fair share of the load?

_____

_____

_____

What should be done with non-performers? Why? Whose responsibility is it?

_____

_____

_____

ZERO DEFECTS

Is 99% good enough?

Is "good enough" good enough for the 21st century? The well worn saying, "If it ain't broke, don't fix it" may be a broken statement, itself in need of repair.

Certainly, in the 20th century there was a time when customers would tolerate mediocre products. There was a time when you may have even expected to take in your new car several times until all of the problems were corrected.

167

Then in the late 20th century Japanese companies brought their improved version of quality to United States markets. Products were right the first time, every time. The standard of excellence had been set and customers expected zero defects as an everyday occurrence. Then nearly all the wrist watches, cassette players and VCR's sold in the United States came from Japan. To add to the excellence, zero defects were achieved while costs were lowered.

ZERO

ZIP

ZILCH

NOTHING

NIL

NONE

By the end of the 20th century, products that performed flawlessly and were less expensive than the year before became the norm. Perhaps the best example is television sets that were bigger, sharper, and packed with more options that became less expensive each year.

Now as we begin the 21st century, the automotive companies and their suppliers have determined that "good enough" isn't and are striving for, and frequently achieving, six sigma levels of quality. That is 99.9997% perfect or no more than three defective parts per million, and zero defects per million is a result that is being achieved.

Did you know that if doctors were only 99% accurate, more than 23,000 people would be incorrectly pronounced dead in the United States each year? Can we agree that in some areas of life (and death), only perfection is good enough?

How good do you need to be? As good as a heart beat? If your heart beats 72 times a minute, that is 103,680 times per day. That amounts to 37,843,200 beats per year. If your heart were only 99% accurate, you would skip 378,432 beats a year!

Your heart wouldn't beat for 13,140 seconds or 219 minutes per year, if only 99% accurate.

Hearts don't skip beats like that and live for long. Neither do companies that don't achieve zero defects.

Remember, zero defects is not just some abstract search for excellence that is beyond reach. If your company can't get to zero defects, perhaps your competition will.

ZERO is today's reality.

How would you feel standing on the edge of a cliff wearing a set of glider wings that were almost defect free?

Questions

What percentage of your production is defective on a daily basis? Monthly?

_____

_____

_____

What could you do to improve these numbers?

_____

_____

_____

What programs are in place for employees to work together formally to improve their work processes to prevent defects?

_____

_____

_____

What are you doing to make yourself 99.9997% defect free?

_____

_____

_____

Closing Thoughts

As a child, I remember sitting at our small kitchen table, eating dinner each evening and listening to my father complain about work and the people he had to work with. Every day. Eventually, the company was sold and he and many other employees were let go. A few years later, the company closed. He had been there 34 years.

Now, at 82, he still reminisces about work, remembering the disagreements and conflicts that were part of his routine.

I wish instead he had stories to tell of success and helping others grow and of happy pride-filled times of team accomplishments. He doesn't.

For much of the 20th century, arguments, adversarial relationships, layoffs and then eventual plant closings were all part of work.

Perhaps the 21st century holds something better. Do you also hope that work will be something you get to do, rather than have to do? Do you also hope that work will be a place of pride of accomplishment, of camaraderie and of personal fulfillment? You and others can make it that way.

Most important, I hope that your 21st century dinner-table conversations about work are far more positive and uplifting than they were for many of us who grew up in the 20th century. You and your children deserve the best of the 21st century.

As you get ready to close this book, I encourage you to open it again and again to use it as an aid in making positive changes in you and your Future@Work.

Finally, as you turn to the next and last page, I would like to conclude with some inspiring words by George Washington Carver. His poem, *I Can*, has helped me to start many a day with an "I also can!" attitude.

Now, go take on the century, one day at a time.

I CAN   -- George Washington Carver

Figure it out for yourself, my lad,
You've all the greatest of men have had:
Two arms, two hands, two legs, two eyes,
And a brain to use if you would be wise.
With this equipment they all began.
Do start from the top and say, "I can."

Look them over, the wise and the great;
They take their food from a common plate,
And similar knives and forks they use,
With similar laces, they tie their shoes,
The world considers them brave and smart,
But you've all they had when they made their start.

You can triumph and come to skill,
You can be great if you only will.
You're well equipped for what fight you choose;
You have arms and legs and a brain to use,
And the man who has risen, great deeds to do,
Began his life with no more than you.

You are the handicap you must face;
You are the one who must choose his place,
You must say what you want to do,
How much to study, the truth to know;
God has equipped you for life, but He
Let's YOU decide what you want to be.

Courage must come from the soul within,
The man must furnish the will to win.
So figure it out yourself, my lad;
You were born with all that the great have had;
With your equipment, they all began.
Get a hold of yourself and say: "I CAN!"

About the Author...

Nick Synko has worked in a
variety of management assignments
for more than twenty-five years.

His corporate experience ranges
from manufacturing plants to
corporate offices. His last
corporate assignment was as the
Manager of Executive and
Professional Development
for a 15,000 employee company.

In 1991 he founded Synko & Associates,
a consulting and training firm specializing
in the development of individual, team and
leadership skills.

Current clients range from major
divisions of multi-national firms
to companies of fewer than 100
employees.

Nick has experience in the following
industries and organizations: automotive
manufacturing, biomedical products, medical
devices and supplies, electronics, computer
assembly, oil and gas, metals and non-profit
organizations.

Nick, and his wife Cathy, have four
children and reside in Saline, Michigan.

Nick can be reached at: NSYNKO@AOL.COM

About the Illustrator...

Brian Narelle has been cartooning since the age of eight because no one ever told him to stop.

A graduate of USC Film School, he has directed and animated for Sesame Street, was supervising animator on the Korty/Lucas film feature *Twice Upon a Time* and created the original chicken for San Diego's KGB radio.

As an actor he has starred in John Carpenter's *Dark Star* and TLC's kid's series *Bingo & Molly.*
An award winning screenwriter, his children's films include the *Sooper Puppy, Wizard of No and What Tadoo* series.

Illustrator of *You're a Genius!* by Kimberly Kassner, his cartoons have also appeared in magazines and comics, as well as servicing corporate clients.

Having taught at the Academy of Art in San Francisco, he now tutors privately.

As long as he has a pen... no napkin is safe!

Brian can be reached at: BNARELLE@EARTHLINK.NET

Acknowledgments

I wish to acknowledge the following people for the inspiration and kind thoughts they contributed throughout the various phases of this book's development. Specifically their input in the following areas was invaluable: commenting upon early drafts of the manuscript, editing, marketing advice and access to other employees and individuals -- all of which were instrumental in the book's development.

Many thanks are therefore owed to: Donna Angle, Mike Bethell, Kevin Bingel, Dave Bloomfield, Cathy Bodkins, Arlo Bower, Elizabeth Carlson, Tommy Coppinger, Leora Druckman, Vaughn DuBose, John Duktig, Scott Fenton, JoAnn Gardner, Van Gehl, Dennis Gerlach, Mark Graham, Doug Guthrie, Mike Harper, Robin Hart, John Hermann, Bob Hunter, Al Huth, Tom Hurt, John T. Johnson, Jr., Laurie Beth Jones, Tony Kakuk, Kimberly Kassner, Mark Kenworthy, John Lechman, Wesley A. Lytle, Vic Mahajan, Jeff McCann, Karen Miller, Bob Moawad, Brian Narelle, Gerald Nidiffer, Scott Pohlmann, John Price, David Rollins, Howard Saunders, Glenn Sparschu, Lloyd Sydney, Jean Ward, Dick Waring, Norm Wetzel, Jeff Wilson, Robert Whitely, Donna Winkelman, Gary Yezbick, Joe Yuska, and Margaret Yuska.

A special acknowledgement to my wife and business partner, Cathy, who has spent countless hours listening, advising and editing. Without her support and contributions, this book would have remained only an idea.

Future@Work   ORDER INFORMATION

Hickory Street Press
PO Box 823
3572 Oak Park Drive
Saline, Michigan (MI) 48176-9363 USA

Phone: 734-944-4488

New in 2002 - Available Now!

The Future@Work
Workplace Workbook

Coming in late 2002

The Future@Work
School-To-Work Workbook

Visit our website for further information

www.FutureAtWork.com

Have you ordered a copy
of Future@Work for each
employee at your facility?

Do you have a supply
on hand for new employees?

Do you know students about
to enter the workforce?

Future@Work
makes the perfect
graduation gift.